Berlin

POLAND

EAST
GERMANY

Prague

WEST
GERMANY

CZECHOSLOVAKIA

SOVIET
UNION

AUSTRIA

HUNGARY

HOME

Prague

Distributed in Canada by Douglas & McIntyre Ltd.

Printed and bound in the United States of America by Phoenix Color Corporation

Designed by Robbin Gourley

First edition, 2007

5   7   9   10   8   6   4

www.fsgkidsbooks.com

Library of Congress Cataloging-in-Publication Data

Sís, Peter, date.

The wall : growing up behind the Iron Curtain / Peter Sís.— 1st ed.

p.   cm.

ISBN-13: 978-0-374-34701-7

ISBN-10: 0-374-34701-8

1. Sís, Peter, date—Childhood and youth—Juvenile literature.   2. Illustrators—United States—Biography—Juvenile literature.   3. Authors, American—20th century—Biography—Juvenile literature.   4. Czech Americans—Biography—Juvenile literature.   5. Czechoslovakia—Social conditions—1945–1992—Juvenile literature.   6. Czechoslovakia—History—1945–1992—Juvenile literature.   I. Title.

NC975.5.S57A2 2007

943.704092—dc 22

[B]

2006049149

The four propaganda posters that appear on the first journal spread come from
Power of Images, Images of Power (Prague, 2005), courtesy Galerie U Křižovníků, Prague.

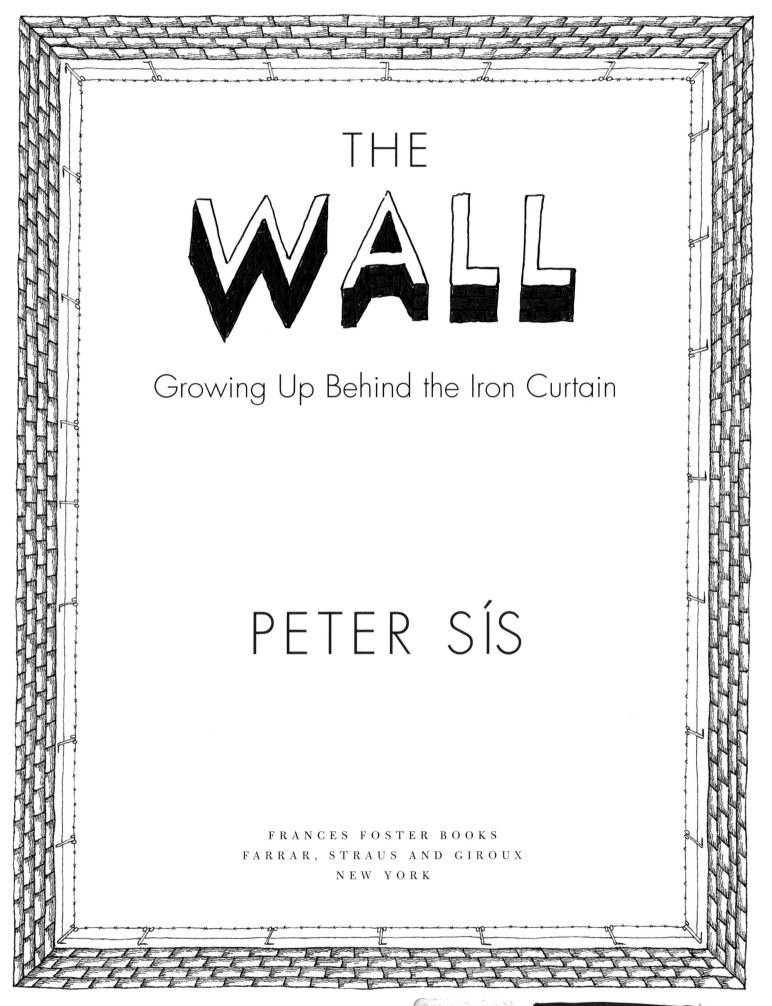

THE
WALL

Growing Up Behind the Iron Curtain

PETER SÍS

FRANCES FOSTER BOOKS
FARRAR, STRAUS AND GIROUX
NEW YORK

INTRODUCTION

WE DON'T HAVE TO GO FAR BACK IN TIME TO SEE THAT THE MAP OF THE world keeps changing. In the twentieth century alone, the changes were often cataclysmic. In 1917, the Russian Empire was swept by a revolution that brought the Communist Party to power and established the Soviet Union.

At the end of World War I in 1918, the Austro-Hungarian Empire fell apart and several countries gained independence. Czechoslovakia was one of them. But after two decades of democracy, Czechoslovakia was taken over by Nazi Germany. Then, in 1939, World War II erupted. The Allies—the United States, Britain, France, and the Soviet Union—defeated Germany and Japan in 1945 and liberated the countries that Germany had occupied.

After the war, responsibility for governing these countries was divided between the Allied forces. Most of eastern Europe and the eastern part of Germany fell under Russian control and became known as the Eastern Bloc. The rest of Germany was in the Western Bloc, led by the United States.

The Soviet Union and the Western nations managed their territories in very different ways. The Western Bloc countries were all independent democracies, while the Eastern Bloc was tightly controlled by the Soviet Union. But not everyone in the Eastern Bloc countries wanted to live under totalitarian dictatorships, and many people began leaving for the West. To prevent a mass exodus, the Soviet Union fortified the borders around much of Eastern Europe and eventually built a wall that cut the city of Berlin in half. And so Europe was divided—symbolically, ideologically, and physically—by what Winston Churchill, the British statesman, called an Iron Curtain.

By the 1950s, the United States and the Soviet Union each had nuclear weapons, but both sides knew that using them to fight another war would be devastating, and for the next forty years the two superpowers coexisted in a tense standoff, avoiding all-out war. This period was called the Cold War. It lasted until the Berlin Wall fell and the Soviet Empire collapsed. I was born at the beginning of it all, on the Red side—the Communist side—of the Iron Curtain.

—P.S.

As long as he could remember, he had loved to draw.

1948.
The Soviets take
control of
Czechoslovakia
and close the
borders.

The People's
Militia enforces
the new order.

At first he drew shapes.

Communist symbols and monuments appear everywhere.

The Czech government takes its orders from Moscow.

The display of red flags on state holidays— **COMPULSORY**. *People who don't comply are punished.*

Then he drew people.

The Communists take control of the schools.

Russian-language classes— **COMPULSORY**.

Joining the Young Pioneers, the Communist youth movement— **COMPULSORY**.

Political indoctrination— **COMPULSORY**.

Collecting scrap metal— **COMPULSORY**.

First of May parade celebrating the workers of the world— **COMPULSORY**.

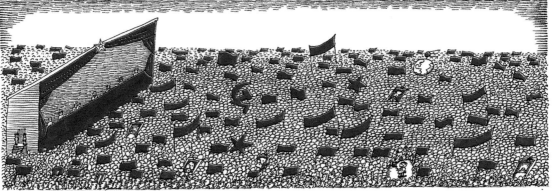

After drawing whatever he wanted to at home,

Public displays of loyalty— **COMPULSORY.**

The practice of religion— **DISCOURAGED.**

Children are encouraged to report on their families and fellow students. Parents learn to keep their opinions to themselves.

Citizens participate in the Spartakiad—a mass gymnastics exercise glorifying individual subordination to socialist ideals— **COMPULSORY.**

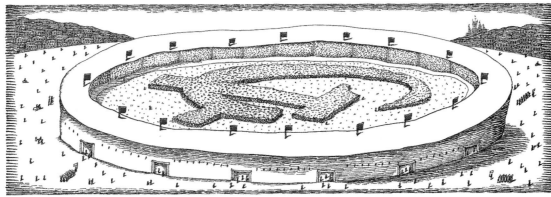

he drew what he was told to at school.

Hungary 1956. A popular uprising is crushed by the Soviet Union.

Germany 1961. The Berlin Wall is erected by the Soviets to keep East Berliners from defecting to the West. It cuts the city in half.

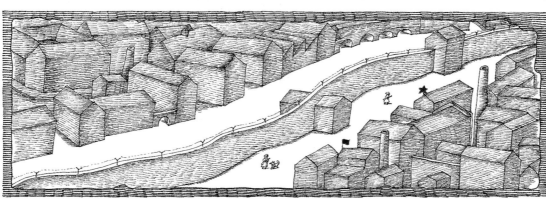

The Iron Curtain separating East and West is strengthened, and the Cold War escalates.

He drew tanks.

October 1962. Soviet missiles in Cuba are aimed at the United States. Nuclear war is narrowly averted.

June 26, 1963. President John F. Kennedy visits the Berlin Wall and declares, "Ich bin ein Berliner— I am a Berliner."

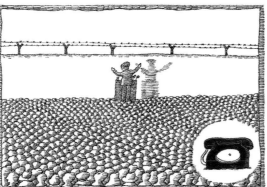

November 22, 1963. President Kennedy is assassinated in Dallas, Texas.

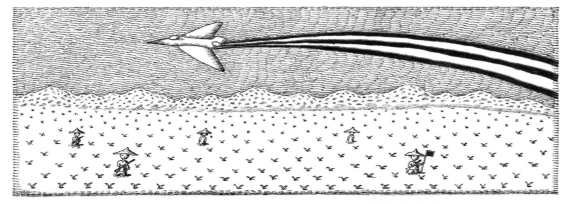

The United States and Communists fight in Vietnam.

Nuclear war is a constant threat.

He drew wars.

Czechoslovak students help farmers fight a potato beetle infestation. The beetles are blamed on the U.S.A.

Secret police are watching everyone.

Students harvest hops (used for brewing beer).

Russian films glorifying Soviet ideals are shown regularly to schoolchildren.

The Great Socialistic October Revolution is celebrated annually on November 7 by a nighttime march.

All of the above— **COMPULSORY**.

He didn't question what he was being told.

Telephones are bugged.

Display of Western flags— **PROHIBITED**.

Only the official art, Socialist Realism, is permitted.

Certain books and films are banned. Art and culture are censored.

Western radio is banned (and jammed).

Letters are opened and censored.

Informers are rewarded for snooping.

There are shortages of almost everything. People stand in long lines.

OVOCE ZELENINA

Then he found out there were things he wasn't told.

GAGARIN

LAIKA

KHR

AURORA

LENIN

THIS WAS THE TIME OF BRAINWASHING.

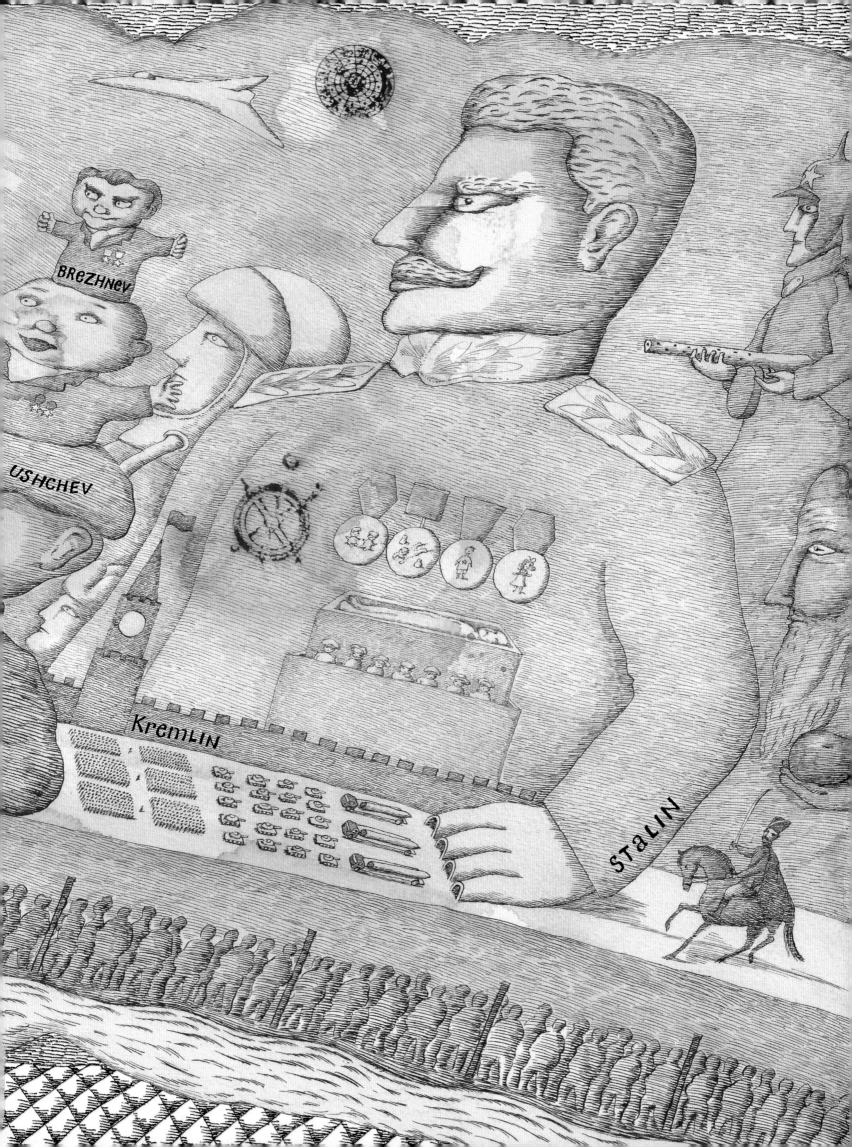

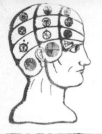

FROM MY JOURNALS

1954

My father has been drafted into the Army Film Unit. They sent him to China to make a film.

We're supporting world peace by not eating meat on Thursdays.

We are all encouraged to get a pen pal in the Soviet Union. I've chosen Volodja in Leningrad. Our letters are graded.

April 1956

My father's cousin Lamin is in prison as an enemy of the state. My grandmother talks to my parents about it in German so my sister and I won't understand. But we understand some of it. He was on a national volleyball team that was going to a tournament in the West, and the players were all planning to stay there. The secret police found out. Lamin is twenty years old and will be in prison for the rest of his life.

February 1957

We went on a skiing vacation in the mountains on the western border. Soldiers with dogs came through the train looking for "subversives" trying to cross the border. The soldiers checked our skis and told us if we saw anyone who looked suspicious or behaved strangely, we should tell. When we got off the train, there were two extra pairs of skis, and two people were missing!

November 3, 1957

The Soviet Union launched a rocket carrying a little dog named Laika into space. I wonder how the dog is going to land?

1958

We were given our Young Pioneer scarves at the Lenin Museum in Prague—all except Dežo Hlaváč because he is from a Gypsy family with "too many children" and is not considered ready.

March 1959

There is a story in our schoolbook about a Russian man who is a class enemy. He hides his wheat harvest in his cellar instead of giving it to the village cooperative. His son, who is a Young Pioneer, finds out and reports it. The family kills the boy. His name is Pavka Morozov. He is a hero. We are told that if we see our parents doing wrong, we should report them.

June 1960

We are rehearsing for the Spartakiad. I'm in the ten-to-twelve-year-old group. Our part is called "Joyous Spring." We wear green shorts and yellow shirts. Each age group has its own segment and different uniform colors. The women are spectacular, and the soldiers are the most daring.

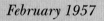

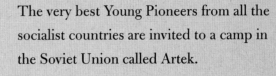
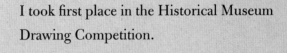
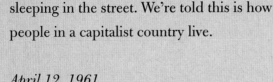

1961

We watch an American movie called *On the Bowery* at school. It shows poor people sleeping in the street. We're told this is how people in a capitalist country live.

April 12, 1961

The Soviet Union launched the first man into space, Yuri Gagarin. When he returned, he landed safely in Siberia.

April 28, 1961

We welcome cosmonaut Yuri Gagarin to Prague. I wish he had brought his dog Laika with him.

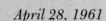

June 17, 1962

The Czechoslovak National Soccer Team plays Brazil in the World Cup soccer championship final in Chile. We lose.

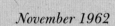

November 1962

Every May we stand guard at the giant Stalin statue. But now the statue has been blown up. We will stand guard at the smaller monuments . . .

There is a five-year plan for the whole country. We are building socialism. America is a capitalist country. So are France, Britain, Italy, and Holland. But my schoolbook tells me that America is the most capitalistic and decadent of all.

The very best Young Pioneers from all the socialist countries are invited to a camp in the Soviet Union called Artek.

I took first place in the Historical Museum Drawing Competition.

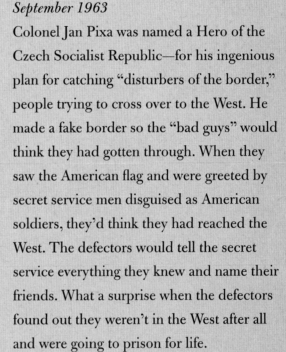

September 1963

Colonel Jan Pixa was named a Hero of the Czech Socialist Republic—for his ingenious plan for catching "disturbers of the border," people trying to cross over to the West. He made a fake border so the "bad guys" would think they had gotten through. When they saw the American flag and were greeted by secret service men disguised as American soldiers, they'd think they had reached the West. The defectors would tell the secret service everything they knew and name their friends. What a surprise when the defectors found out they weren't in the West after all and were going to prison for life.

    Colonel Pixa is a hero.

I built a scooter that collapsed when my sister, Hana, was riding it downhill. She hates me!

My school visited the Mausoleum to view the embalmed body of the first working-class Communist President of Czechoslovakia, Comrade Klement Gottwald. It was scary.

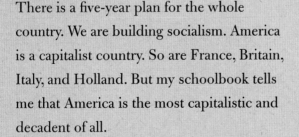

PETR

Bits and pieces of news from the West begin to slip through the Iron Curtain.

The Beatles! (Which one is which?)

Elvis, the Rolling Stones, Radio Luxembourg . . . We secretly tape songs.

Everything from the West seems colorful and desirable.

Citizens age fifteen and over must carry a photo I.D. at all times— **COMPULSORY.**

Slowly he started to question. He painted what he wanted to—in secret.

There are no records, no instruments, no stylish clothes. We have to make and invent everything. We all want to be Beatles.

We make our own shoes, shades, electric guitars . . .

Long hair is a sign of Western decadence. Police have orders to cut it.

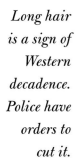

Rock music is against the principles of Socialist art.

He joined a rock group and painted music.

January 1968. The new head of the Communist government, Alexander Dubček, has good intentions.

Slowly, our world begins to open up.

Censorship is lifted.

The old guard and the police are nervous.

Everything seemed possible . . .

It was the Prague Spring of 1968!

The Beatles

film

Harlem GlobeTrotters

aLLen GINSBErG

THEATER

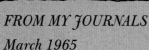

FROM MY JOURNALS

March 1965

I take a walk by the river in the falling snow and pass a black man with a smiley face. He nods. Later, I see a poster and realize I've seen Louis Armstrong, Satchmo. He's in Prague to give a concert!

May 1965

Allen Ginsberg, the American beat poet, comes to Prague. Students make him our Kral Majales (King of May). Then the secret police accuse him of subversion and deport him.

August 1965

A U.S. college all-star basketball team plays in Prague. The best players are some twins and Bill Bradley.

November 1965

The Party newspaper mentions this wild woman called Elvis Presley. It turns out she's a he.

March 1966

My dad came back from France with a 45 single by the Beatles—"A Hard Day's Night."

May 1966

A group of guys with long hair meet in front of the National Museum and get chased by the police. When they are caught, the police pull out scissors and give them haircuts.

Summer 1966

I'm trying to let my hair grow, which is not appreciated at home or at school. My friends and I are learning about the Rolling Stones, Fats Domino, Chuck Berry, rock 'n' roll.

More music, records, and tapes become available. The Harlem Globetrotters are coming to Prague.

December 1966

At first blue jeans are permitted as a uniform of the working classes (but only people with relatives in the West or those with hard currency who can shop in the special store TUZEX are lucky enough to have them). Then the government changes its mind. Jeans are a sign of Western decadence.

February 1967

I form a rock group with my friends, but we have no instruments and we haven't settled on a name yet.

My father makes me get a haircut. I paint people with long hair.

May 1967

We start making instruments. It's hard to make an electric guitar. You plug it into the radio and it blows a fuse.

June 1967

We play songs by the Rolling Stones, Them, Small Faces, the Troggs. My friend Zdenek is an amazing guitarist.

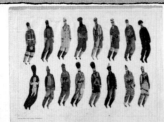

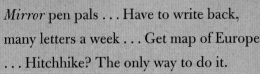

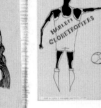

August 1967

Hop-picking time again—a good way to meet girls. After working all day, we get together and sing Beatles songs.

September 1967

There's a rumor that travel restrictions will be lifted. If I can get an invitation from a family in England or Western Europe, I can apply for a passport. I've written to the *Record Mirror,* a magazine in London that has a pen pal column. I sent a photo and a list of my favorite groups.

October 1967

Our group, which we've named New Force, gives a concert at the Central Puppet Theater. The stage is so small there is no room for the drummer. I meet Alena.

    I need boots with heels. Expensive! (Get money from Grandma?)

November 1967

A date with Alena. We walk up and down Wenceslaus Square.

    I draw comics for the school magazine, like those I've seen from San Francisco.

    Make posters for a rock club called Olympic. Hurray!

January 1968

Dubček elected First Secretary of the Party. Gives a speech about freedom!

February 1968

Hundreds of letters arrive from *Record Mirror* pen pals . . . Have to write back, many letters a week . . . Get map of Europe . . . Hitchhike? The only way to do it.

March 1968

A rally for Dubček! We all march. He is calling for "socialism with a human face."

May 1968

Censorship is lifted! We can have long hair and wear jeans! But our school magazine is shut down. The principal complains of anarchy.

June 1968

I've learned how to tie-dye shirts and am getting pretty good at it. I tie-dye everything I can get my hands on.

    The government archives are being opened. I was never told that my uncle Vladimir died in the Communist Leopoldov Prison. The guards killed him. My parents kept this news from us kids.

    We hold a poetry slam at school on the main staircase!

    I have my passport with permission to travel to the West. Yippee! I'll go by train to Paris, cross the Channel, hitchhike to London and Liverpool . . . meet the Beatles?

    The Soviet Union is planning big maneuvers all over Czechoslovakia this summer.

Summer 1968

I'm leaving for England! Back in August with records and posters and pictures . . .

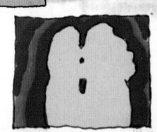

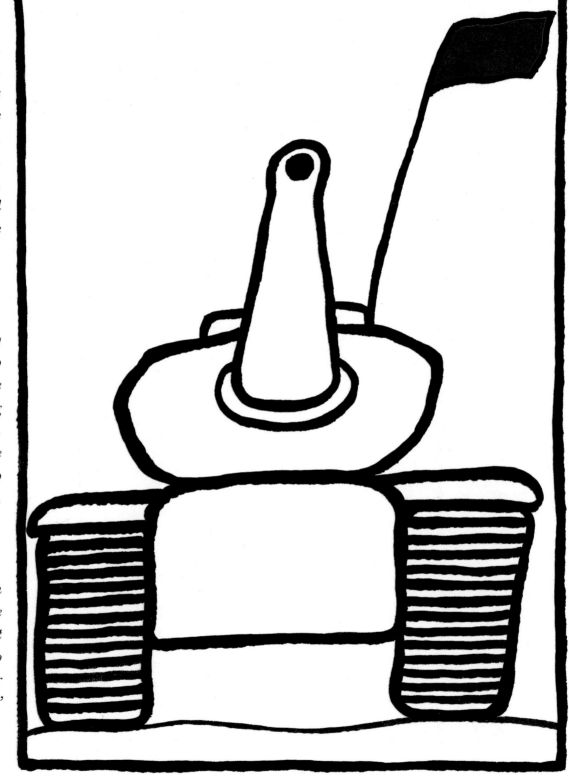

August 21, 1968. 500,000 troops from the Soviet Union, Bulgaria, East Germany, Hungary, and Poland invade Czechoslovakia.

Ordinary citizens try to persuade the invading soldiers to leave. They change street signs to confuse them.

The Czech progressive government is sent to Moscow for "reeducation."

Help from the West doesn't come.

Then—it was all over.

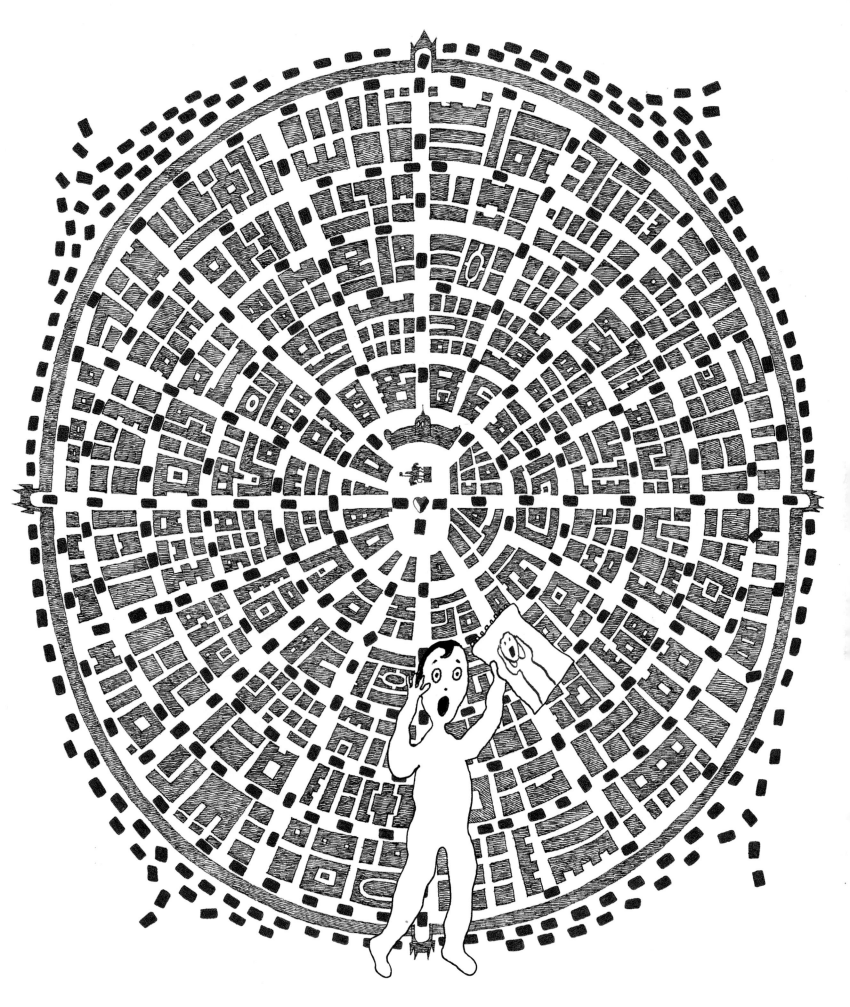

Russian tanks were everywhere.

Ten months after the Soviet invasion, the Beach Boys are invited to Czechoslovakia to give rock concerts.

Rock music fans will be together under one roof.

But out of the dark came a glimmer of hope.

June 17, 1969.
The Prague
concert takes place
in Lucerna Hall.

Police with dogs
wait nearby.

The Beach Boys arrived. America to the rescue!

He was painting dreams . . .

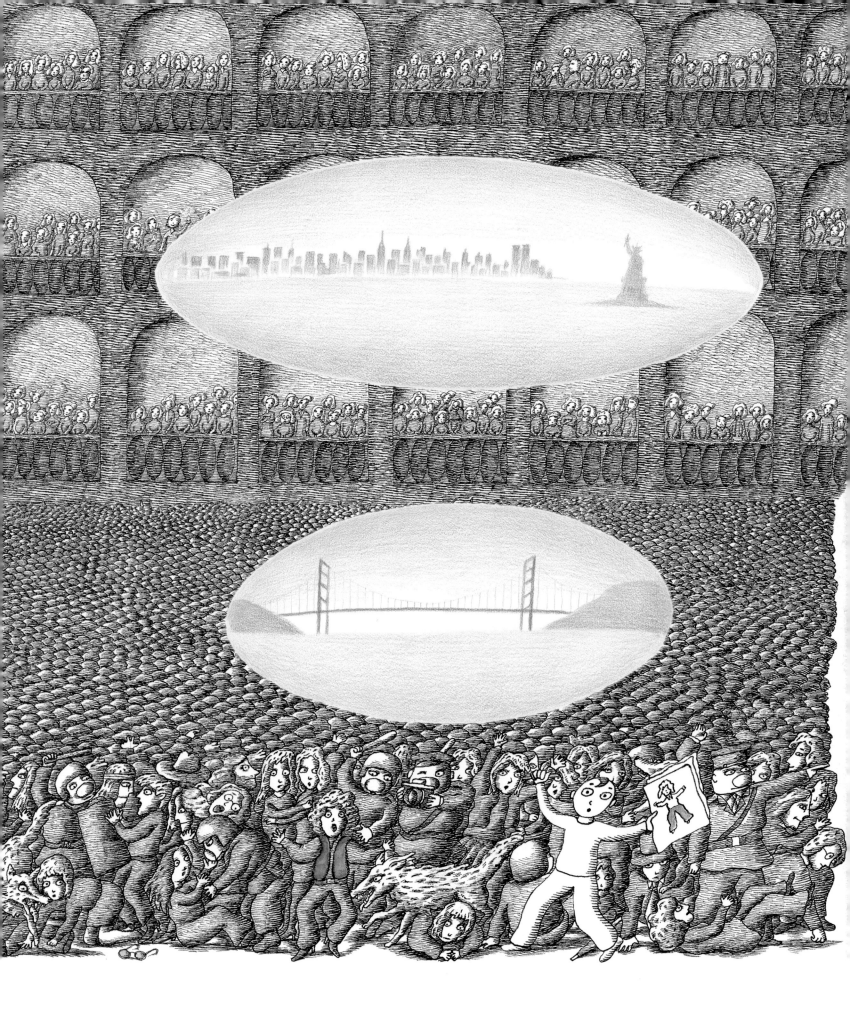

and then nightmares.

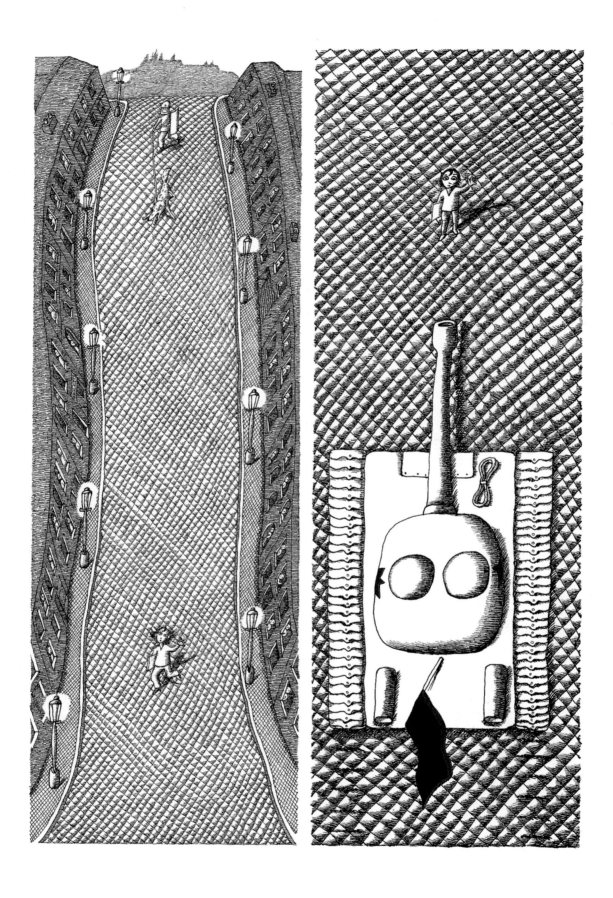

The dreams could be kept to himself,

Anyone considered a threat to the new order is interrogated.

but the drawings could be used against him.

The Iron Curtain descends again.

Alexander Dubček is replaced as head of government.

The secret police provoke riots so the government can exercise tighter controls.

Military service— **COMPULSORY**.

He stopped drawing and was left with only his dreams.

Phones are bugged again, mail opened, people watched.

Western-style art is banned again. Free radio stations are jammed again.

Banned books are secretly translated, copied, and circulated as samizdat.

Discotheques are a new source of information about popular culture.

But he had to draw. Sharing the dreams gave him hope.

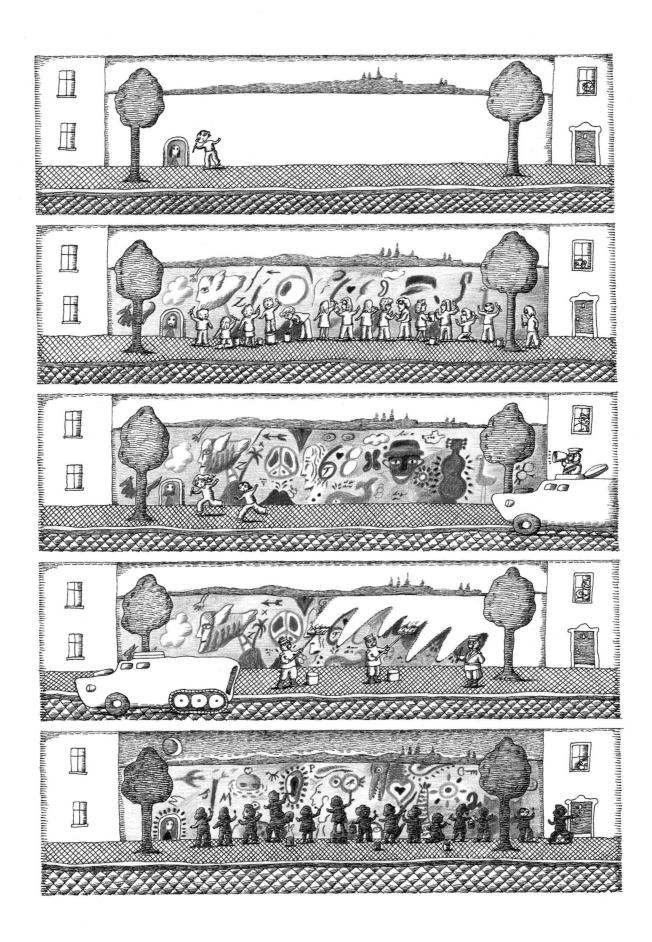

Everyone wanted to draw. They painted a wall filled with their dreams . . .

and repainted it again and again.

FROM MY JOURNALS

January–February 1969
Jan Palach and Jan Zajíc, students, set themselves on fire to "wake up the nation from lethargy."

1970
Větvička, a fun guy and bass player, died of head injuries after the police beat him in the melee following the Beach Boys concert.

1971
My professor at the Academy of Applied Arts, Adolf Hoffmeister (who wrote *Brundibár*), is stripped of his professorship. Anyone considered progressive is replaced.

1972
The border has closed again. Travel is impossible. Goodbye, swinging London!

June 8, 1972
A group of young people with long hair—I know them well—hijack a plane to West Germany. They shoot the pilot with a gun hidden in a baby's diaper.

February 1973
Every one of us in the academy has to create a piece of art celebrating the Soviet Army. I'm glad I'm in the animation department! I'll just paint the backgrounds and explain that the tanks are coming later.

1974
Graduation . . . We're told that our generation is not to be trusted and has no future because we are "tainted" by the events of 1968.

To get a permit to have a studio in my own house, I have to prove that I am an artist in good "social standing," that is, a member of the Communist Party. The curious thing is that I have just been offered a position as an assistant professor in the academy. I am told I am the youngest ever to be considered. I am elated, but then comes the condition: I must join the Party. They promise me that no one has to know about it! Thanks, but no thanks. I draw small pictures. I do not need a studio.

1975
My first professional assignment—an album cover for Karel Černoch's *Letiště* (*Airport*). I paint a little airport with a red-and-white wind sock blowing in the wind. "Did you check which direction the wind sock is blowing?" the art director asks. I laugh, thinking he's joking. "It's very important," he says, "an ideological issue." If the wind is blowing from west to east, it could be read as coming from West Germany to the Soviet Union. Ideological diversion. Infiltration. He calls the Ministries of Culture and the Interior. We wait for them to call back. "You're in luck!" says the art director. "Your wind is blowing in the right direction."

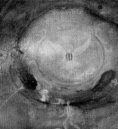

1975–76

Army service.

Rock bands can no longer perform without a permit.

All artists now have to prove their social and political qualifications.

1976

The Plastic People of the Universe rock band are in prison. I used to argue with them, and do not care for their music—but prison?

January 1977

Dissidents formed an organization called Charter 77. As a result, some of them are in prison. Some have been threatened and tortured, stripped of citizenship, and driven with their families to the western border and kicked out of the country.

January 28, 1977

Prominent artists, writers, film directors, actors, and musicians were invited to the National Theater for a "celebration." When they were all in the theater, the doors were locked, and they were instructed to sign a document supporting the "fraternal help of the Soviet Army" in 1968 (that is, the invasion). Most signed.

Bad news/good news—my dad is in the hospital. He couldn't attend. I'm almost sure he wouldn't have signed . . . What would I have done?

May 1977

Finally, my first professional film: an animated fairy tale, *Island for 6,000 Alarm Clocks* by Miloš Macourek. The story: 6,000 alarm clocks feel beaten down and unappreciated and walk off the job. They walk and walk until they get to a little island where they can ring as they please.

I spend a year painting, cutting, animating. The film looks great, all ten minutes of it. Everyone congratulates me. Then the censors decide that the film gives the wrong message by suggesting that you can walk away if you don't like something. Was I telling people to emigrate? People are always looking for hidden messages.

There is a whole science to learn about dealing with censors. You have to give them something to change. For instance, if you're making a film or a painting, or writing a book or a song, you put in a big church. You can be sure the censors will tell you to take it out, and perhaps they won't notice the smaller, important things. Theater people have the "little white dog" theory. If you let a little white dog parade across the front of the stage, the censors won't notice what is happening in the background.

June 1977

Rumors, rumors, rumors. Everyone suspects everyone else of being an informer.

Can we hope things are ever going to get better?

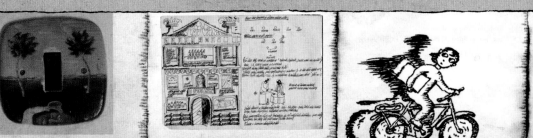

Very few dare to stand up and criticize the government.

Jan Palach protests the regime.

Dissident playwright Václav Havel is jailed.

Everyone has to prove loyalty to the Soviet system.

Things got worse . . .

Artists are brought to the National Theater under false pretenses.

Dissidents are forced to do menial jobs.

A doctor

A professor

People are followed, monitored, harassed, imprisoned, deported, and tortured.

and worse.

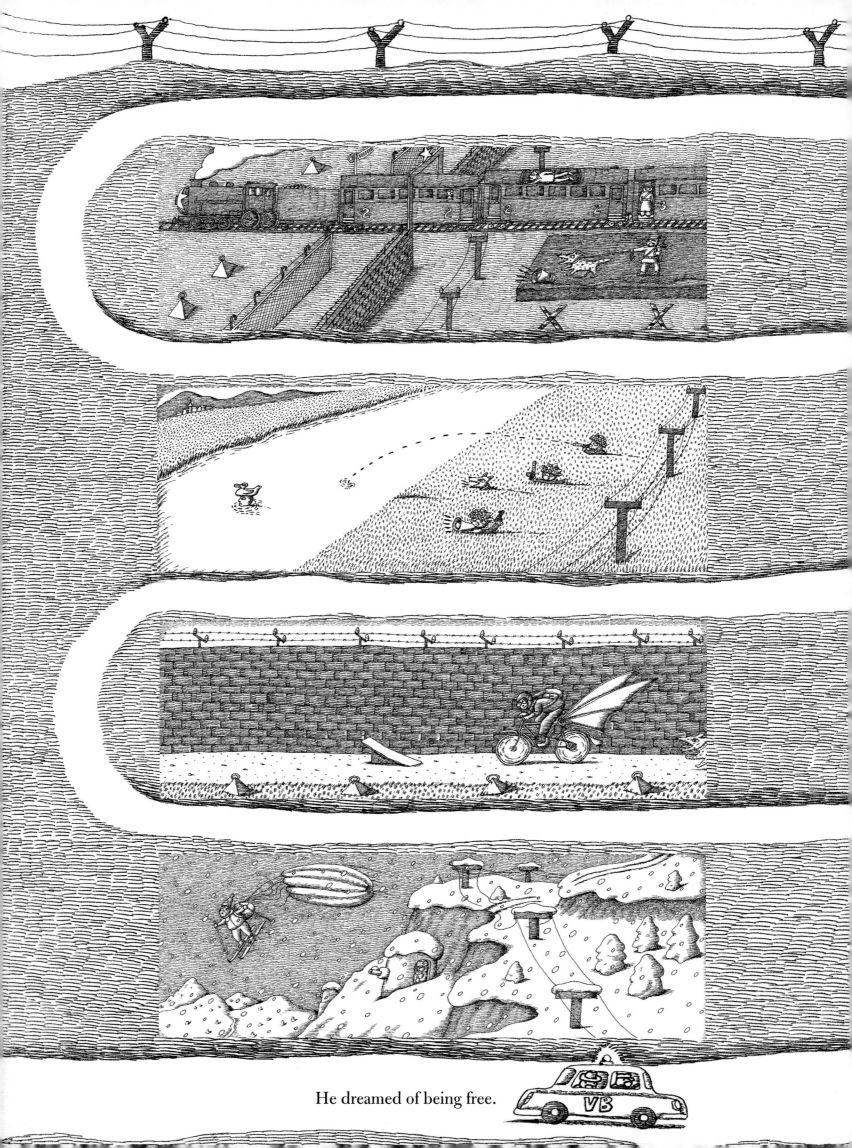

He dreamed of being free.

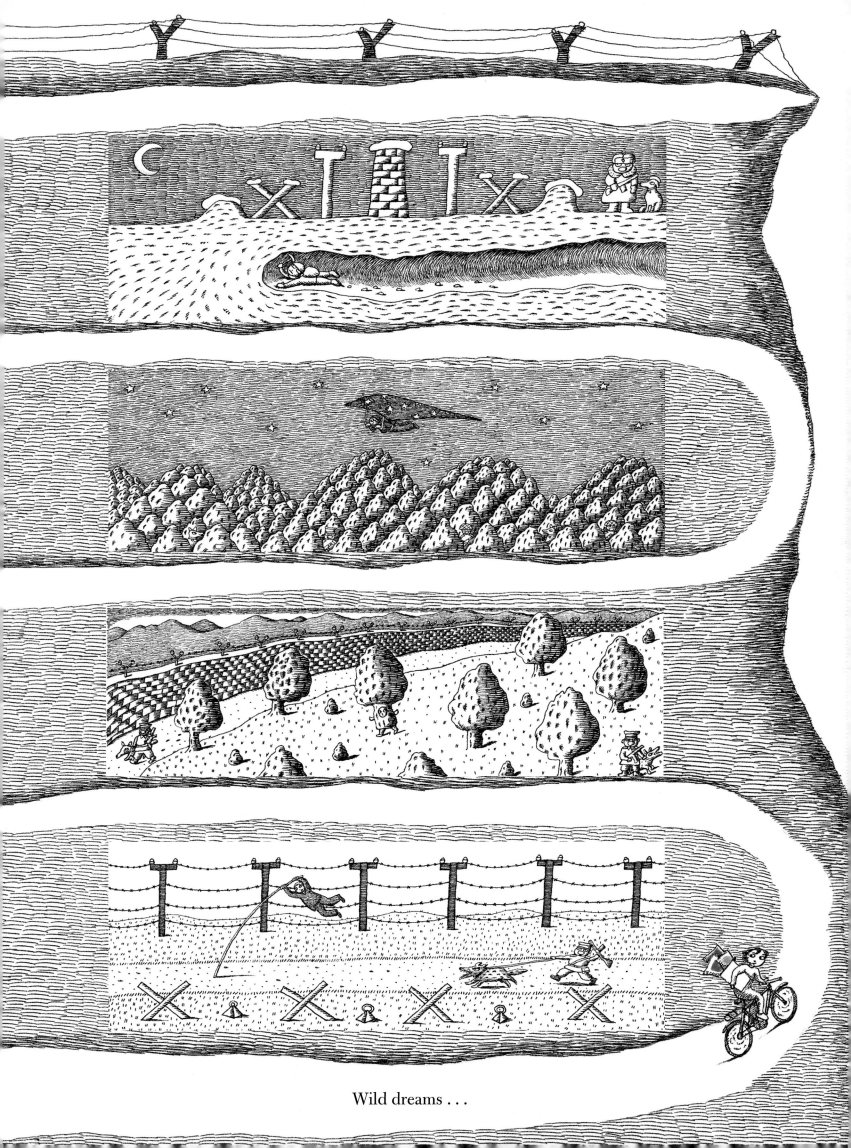

Wild dreams . . .

These ideas spread throughout Eastern Europe and lead to the fall of the Wall and the collapse of the Communist system.

In the mid-1980s, Mikhail Gorbachev recognizes the need to open up the rigid Soviet system and introduces the policies of perestroika (restructuring) and glasnost (openness).

SOMETIMES DREAMS COME TRUE.

One country after another becomes free: Poland (1989), Czechoslovakia (1989), Hungary (1989–1990), East Germany (1989–1990), Romania (1989–1990), and Bulgaria (1989–1990). East and West Germany reunite (1990), and the Soviet Union breaks up (1991). The Cold War is over.

ON NOVEMBER 9, 1989, THE WALL FELL.

"ARE YOU A SETTLER, DAD?" MY CHILDREN ASKED WHEN THEY WERE YOUNGER AND WERE learning about America's first settlers. "How did you decide to settle here in America?"

"It was all because of drawing" was my answer.

I do not know if I was born to draw, but we had no television or computers when I was a child, so I drew. I drew stories about my grandfather in the First World War, fighting the Russians for Austria-Hungary, and about my father in Tibet. I drew cowboys and Indians and copied comic strips from the oversize book my other grandfather brought from Chicago, where he designed railroads in the 1920s. In my parents' house I was free to draw whatever I wanted.

All this changed when I started school and became part of the Soviet Communist system. Then I drew what I was told to draw and thought what I was told to think. Looking back, I can see how easy it is to brainwash a child. We were like sheep . . . until music from the free world—rock 'n' roll and the Beatles—made a crack in the wall. Then came more music . . . a bigger crack . . . the Prague Spring . . . and everything seemed possible. I was allowed to travel; I hitchhiked all over Europe and thought the world was my oyster.

I was in London when the Russian tanks rolled into Prague. My family was vacationing in Europe, and we met in Germany to decide whether to return or to leave our country. We went back, naïvely hoping things wouldn't be too bad. And they weren't, at least not right away. I became a disc jockey with a radio program and interviewed famous bands like the Beatles, Led Zeppelin, and The Who. I traveled with the Beach Boys on their mini-tour of Czechoslovakia. But then things got bad. My radio show was canceled and rock music was banned. I threw myself into drawing and painting. I painted chairs, light switches, even the refrigerator at home. It was too scary outside.

I also made animated films, and they opened the world for me again—but not completely. I was allowed to leave the country but always told when to come back. I was working on an animated film in Los Angeles when the Soviets decided to boycott the 1984 Olympics, and I was called back to Prague. This time I resisted. I was tired of being told what to do, what to think, and what to draw . . . but after a lifetime of being brainwashed, it was not an easy decision. I was afraid I might never see my family again. I thought the Soviets would be in power forever.

Now when my American family goes to visit my Czech family in the colorful city of Prague, it is hard to convince them it was ever a dark place full of fear, suspicion, and lies. I find it difficult to explain my childhood; it's hard to put it into words, and since I have always drawn everything, I have tried to draw my life—before America—for them. Any resemblance to the story in this book is intentional.

—P.S.

As long as he can remember, he will continue to draw.